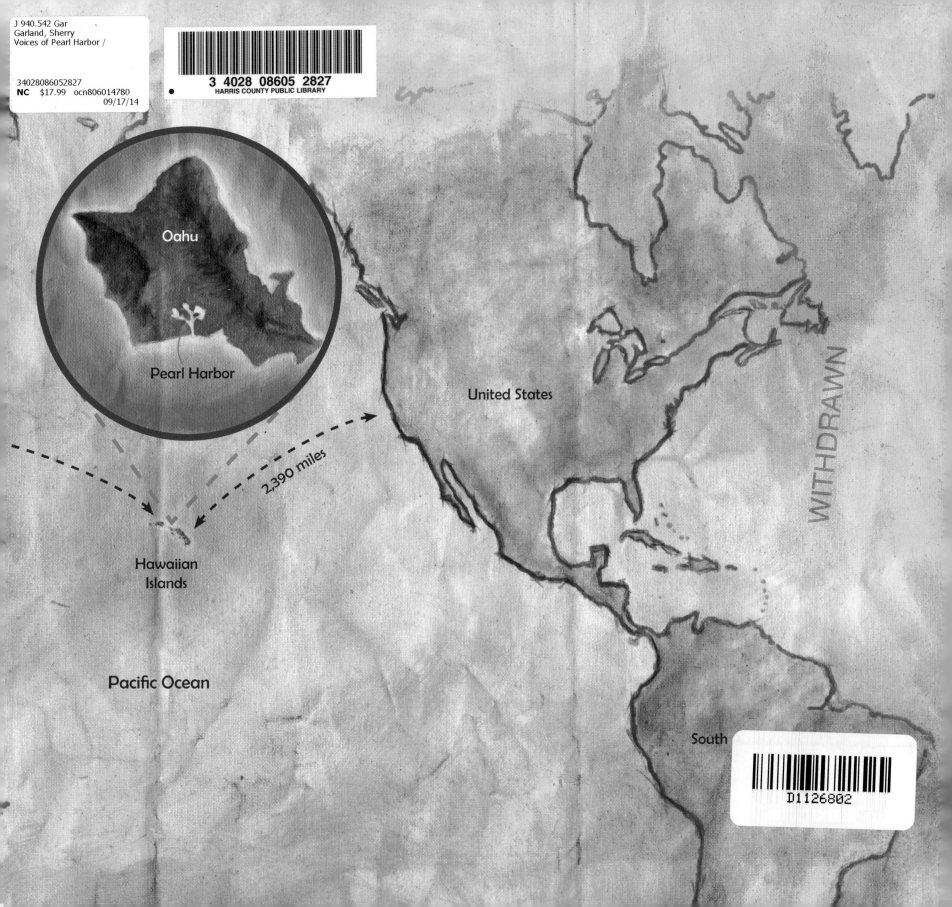

Oahu

Pearl Harbor

United States

2,390 miles

Hawaiian
Islands

Pacific Ocean

South

VOICES of PEARL HARBOR

VOICES of PEARL HARBOR

By Sherry Garland
Paintings by Layne Johnson

PELICAN PUBLISHING COMPANY
Gretna 2013

In memory of my cousin, Olis Denver Camp, US Army 536th Amphibious Tractor Battalion, 7th Infantry, who lost his life on May 21, 1945, age 20, Battle of Okinawa.
—*S. G.*

I would like to thank Elise Chouinard, Wyatt Ferguson, and Lena Scholten. Special thanks to Aileen Kirkham whose father served aboard the USS Tennessee *during the attack. In remembrance of those who honorably gave so much for so many. May their sacrifice never be forgotten.*
—*L. J.*

Acknowledgements

My gratitude goes to the staff of the following historical sites: National Museum of the Pacific War (Fredericksburg, Tex.); USS *Battleship Texas* (Houston, Tex.); USS *Lexington* (Corpus Christi, Tex.); USS *Arizona* Memorial (Pearl Harbor, Hawaii). Special thanks go to Sr. Chief Petty Officer Frank Allison (US Navy, retired), Sr. Chief Petty Officer Fred Allison (US Navy, retired), and Jack Fletcher (US Coast Guard) for their assistance with nautical terminology; and Dorothea "Dee" Buckingham's wonderful Web site "Women of World War II Hawaii." Any errors in this book are solely mine.

The word "Pelican" and the depiction of a pelican are trademarks of Pelican Publishing Company, Inc., and are registered in the U.S. Patent and Trademark Office.

Library of Congress Cataloging-in-Publication Data

Garland, Sherry.
  Voices of Pearl Harbor / by Sherry Garland ; illustrated by Layne Johnson.
    p. cm.
  Includes bibliographical references.
  ISBN 978-1-4556-1609-1 (hardcover : alk. paper) — ISBN 978-1-4556-1610-7 (e-book) 1. Pearl Harbor (Hawaii), Attack on, 1941—Juvenile literature. I. Johnson, Layne, ill. II. Title.
  D767.92.G37 2013
  940.54'26693—dc23

                    2012035072

Disclaimer
Although the events depicted are historically accurate, the words spoken by real historical persons represent the author's creative interpretation of what they might have thought and said. As such, the first person narratives should not be considered to be actual quotations.

Printed in Malaysia
Published by Pelican Publishing Company, Inc.
1000 Burmaster Street, Gretna, Louisiana 70053

Pearl Harbor

O beautiful isles, born of fire,
paradise rising from the crystal sea;
your fragrant air, your soothing surf
patiently awaiting your dark destiny.

Island of Hawaii

1940

I am a native islander born many years ago
in the old Kingdom of Hawaii.
As a lad I dived for pearls in calm blue waters
and watched whaling ships sail by.

Today my beloved isle belongs to America.
Docks and quays and oily ships
fill the places where dolphins used to play.

President Roosevelt just moved the Pacific Fleet here
and now battleships stream by like a parade of blue giants.

Tensions are high with the Empire of Japan,
for they have been invading Asian countries
one by one, taking what they please.
Maybe this display of naval power
will make them think twice
about provoking the Americans.

October 1941

I am the mother of a brave and loyal son of Nippon,
a naval aviator training for a secret mission.

I stand at the railway station with scarlet thread in hand,
asking kind-hearted strangers to add a stitch
to this good luck belt for my honorable son.
When it contains one thousand stitches,
I shall send it to him as a token of our nation's gratitude.

It was not easy to buy the thread and cloth;
products are scarce in my homeland
because of our long-standing war in China.
Now the Americans have stopped trading with us.

Our new prime minister, General Tojo,
says the British and Americans are punishing Japan
for becoming allies with Hitler and Mussolini.
Some say there will be war in the Pacific soon;
that Japan must fight for her divine right to expand.

All I know is that he is my only son.

December 2, 1941

I am Admiral Kimmel, commander of the Pacific Fleet.
I just received word that for days Navy code-breakers
have intercepted no radio communications
from part of the Imperial Japanese Navy—
six of their carriers have vanished into thin air.

The long-running peace talks with Japanese envoys
have not been going well back in the States.
Washington leaders warned us to be wary of saboteurs,
but they do not seem to worry about an attack here
for we are almost four thousand miles from Japan.
Our naval fleet is protected by a shallow harbor
and thousands of soldiers with their artillery and planes.
No wonder Pearl is nicknamed "Gibraltar of the Pacific."

The top brass in Washington thinks Japan will attack
British or Dutch territories or maybe the Philippines.
But Washington does not have to worry about
Japanese warships slipping silently through the night.

December 3, 1941

I am Vice-Admiral Chuichi Nagumo, Imperial Japanese Navy,
commander of this secret "Operation Hawaii" war-fleet
churning through the cold North Pacific Ocean.

Everyone thought Admiral Yamamoto insane
when he first proposed a surprise attack on Pearl Harbor.
But our engineers designed special torpedoes
that will work in the shallow harbor waters
and armor-piercing bombs to crash through steel.

Our aviators trained rigorously for months;
they studied a replica of Oahu and Pearl Harbor
and each crew knows its assigned target by heart.
Now, we enforce radio silence and lights stay off at night,
for our success depends on the element of surprise.

Yesterday I received the message: "Climb Mount Niitaka."
There is no turning back now; we charge full speed ahead
through this empty sea on the way to our destiny.

December 6, 1941

I am a second lieutenant in the Army Nurse Corps
stationed in this paradise called Hawaii.

A bunch of us gals spent a swell afternoon
splashing in the surf, sunning on the beach,
and sipping cool pineapple juice.

Later we got all dolled up and tootled over
to Bloch Recreation Arena to listen to the
final round of the Battle of Music contest.

Bands from several Navy battleships
rocked the joint with swing and jive.
I danced the jitterbug and Lindy Hop
until the bottoms of my feet throbbed.

It's the beginning of the Christmas holiday season—
there will be parties and more parties from here on.
I cannot believe my good luck at being stationed
on this beautiful isle of romance.

December 7, 1941—6:15 A.M.

I am a pilot in the Imperial Japanese Navy.
Last night I wrote my will and farewell letters.
The admiral gave a speech to rouse our spirits,
then we shouted *"banzai!"* for the emperor's long life.

Early this morning, I said my prayers and bathed,
then placed the belt of a thousand stitches
around my waist for good luck.

After the carrier turned into the wind for our launch,
I climbed aboard my Nakajima torpedo bomber,
with wind and spray slamming my face.

At last we are secured inside the cockpit
and it is our turn to take off over the angry sea.
The deck hands wave their caps, cheering us on
toward our target 230 miles away.

I have confidence we will bring victory to Nippon.
Soon the world will know our power
and show us the respect we deserve.

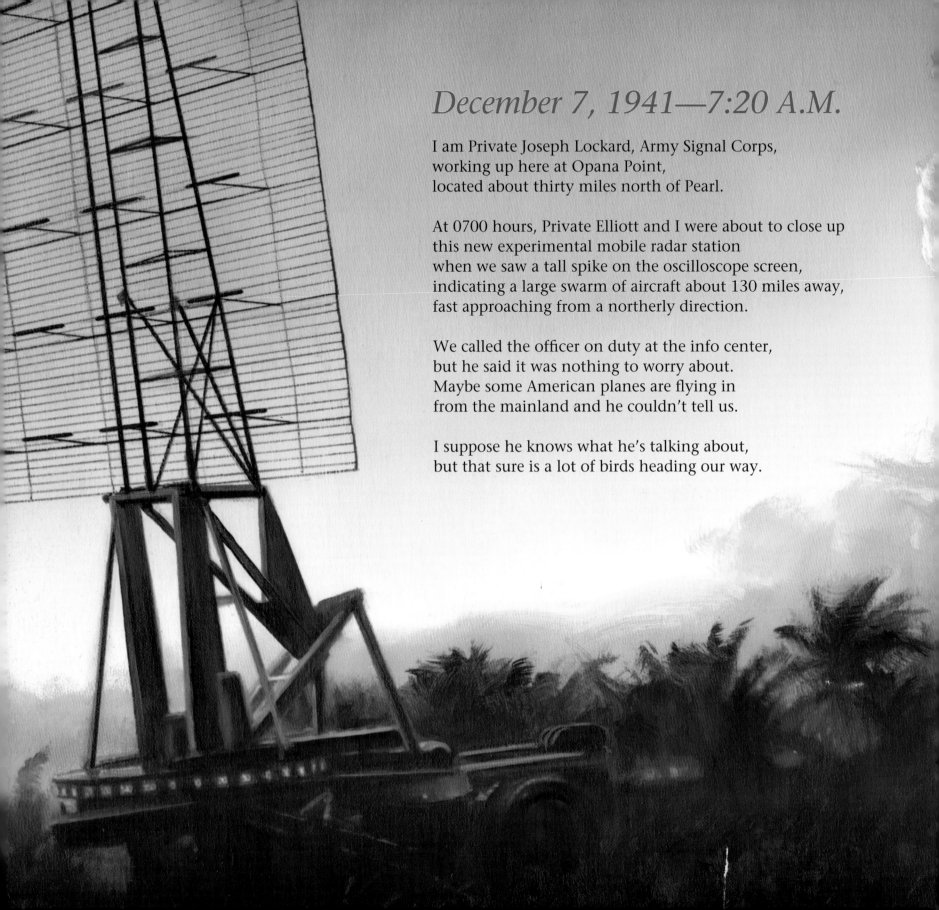

December 7, 1941—7:20 A.M.

I am Private Joseph Lockard, Army Signal Corps,
working up here at Opana Point,
located about thirty miles north of Pearl.

At 0700 hours, Private Elliott and I were about to close up
this new experimental mobile radar station
when we saw a tall spike on the oscilloscope screen,
indicating a large swarm of aircraft about 130 miles away,
fast approaching from a northerly direction.

We called the officer on duty at the info center,
but he said it was nothing to worry about.
Maybe some American planes are flying in
from the mainland and he couldn't tell us.

I suppose he knows what he's talking about,
but that sure is a lot of birds heading our way.

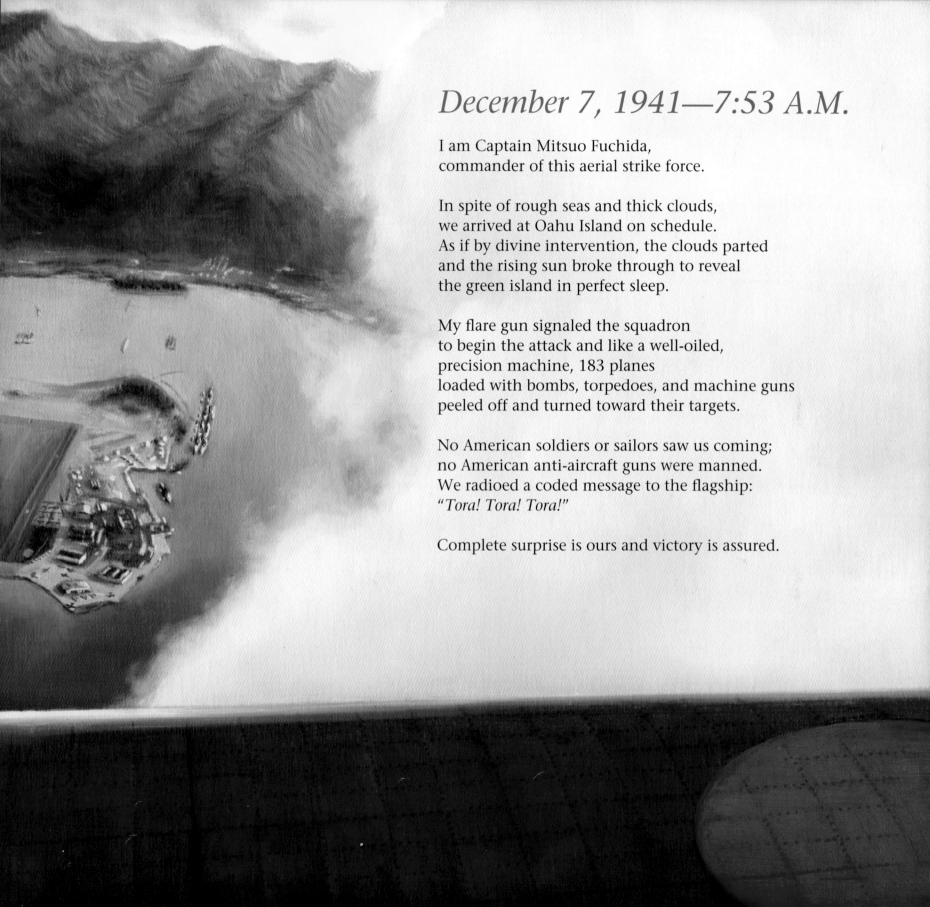

December 7, 1941—7:53 A.M.

I am Captain Mitsuo Fuchida,
commander of this aerial strike force.

In spite of rough seas and thick clouds,
we arrived at Oahu Island on schedule.
As if by divine intervention, the clouds parted
and the rising sun broke through to reveal
the green island in perfect sleep.

My flare gun signaled the squadron
to begin the attack and like a well-oiled,
precision machine, 183 planes
loaded with bombs, torpedoes, and machine guns
peeled off and turned toward their targets.

No American soldiers or sailors saw us coming;
no American anti-aircraft guns were manned.
We radioed a coded message to the flagship:
"Tora! Tora! Tora!"

Complete surprise is ours and victory is assured.

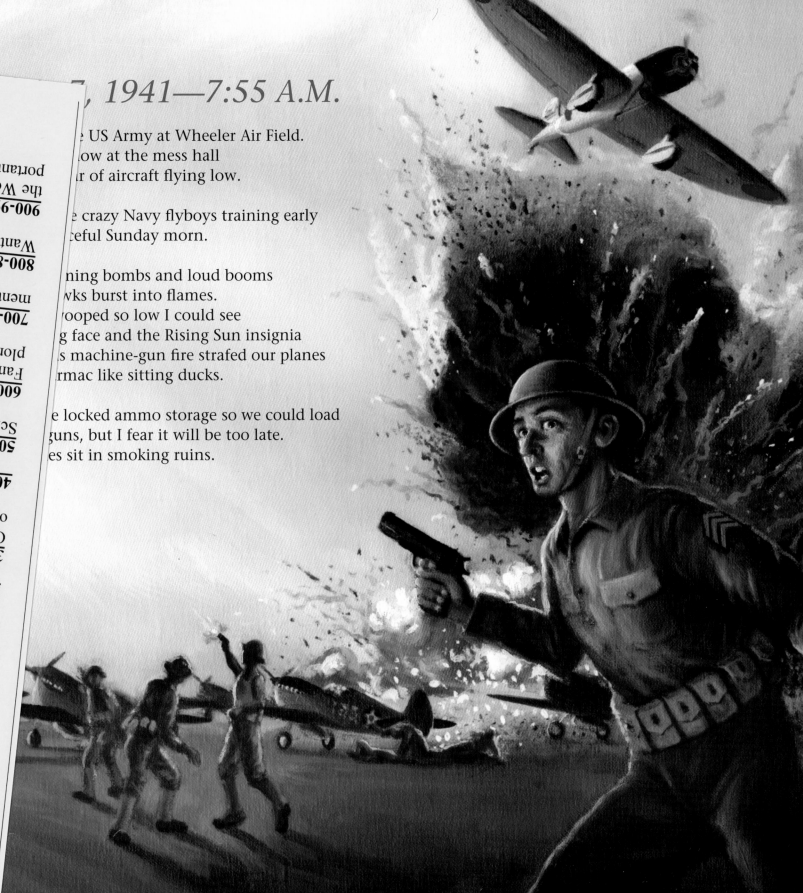

, 1941—7:55 A.M.

e US Army at Wheeler Air Field.
low at the mess hall
r of aircraft flying low.

e crazy Navy flyboys training early
ceful Sunday morn.

ning bombs and loud booms
vks burst into flames.
ooped so low I could see
g face and the Rising Sun insignia
s machine-gun fire strafed our planes
rmac like sitting ducks.

e locked ammo storage so we could load
guns, but I fear it will be too late.
es sit in smoking ruins.

What do those numbers mean ¿

000-099 Information and computers

100-199 Problems, Feelings, Behavior

200-299 Different Beliefs

300-399 People, Laws and Government; Taking Care of our Planet

400-499 The Words We Use

500-599 Birds and Beasts; Science, Space and Math

600-699 Your Body, Your Family, pets, cars, space exploration

700-799 Art & Entertainment and All that Fun Stuff

800-899 I Want to Read! I Want to Write!

900-999 Here and Around the World; History; Important People to Know

December 7, 1941—8:05 A.M.

I am Dorie Miller, mess attendant and
champion boxer on the USS *West Virginia*.

It was almost time for the hoisting of the colors;
the bugler and the Marine color guard were at ready.
The boatswain's mate had just sounded his pipes
when I heard the General Quarters call.

Without warning, torpedoes cut through the water
and hit our ship, while bombs rained from above.
I helped carry the wounded captain to a safer place,
then saw that my battle station was destroyed and
the nearest anti-aircraft gun crew was dead.
I ran to the Browning and grabbed the trigger.
I've never had training on this big ol' 50 caliber gun,
but she's doing a walloping good job.

Shooting at the Japanese Kates and Vals and Zeroes
is like shooting down those pesky squirrels
back in the woods near Waco, when I was a boy.

December 7, 1941—8:10 A.M.

I am a "navy junior," son of a naval officer.
We live on Ford Island in a bungalow on Nob Hill,
tucked right up next to Battleship Row.

I was riding my bicycle when I heard a mess of planes
then saw smoke at Hickam Field across the harbor.
Suddenly loud booms shook the air
as nearby battleships took torpedo hits.

As I raced back toward the house,
I heard a screaming bomb and turned to see
the *Arizona* lift up then explode into roaring flames.
The force blew out the windows of houses
and knocked me to the ground.
Hot shrapnel and debris landed on roofs,
setting some of them ablaze.

Sailors are swimming to shore through raging fires
and through machine gun strafing,
their faces black from oil and burned flesh.

As Mother rushes us to Quarters K for shelter,
I see the mighty *Arizona* starting to go down.

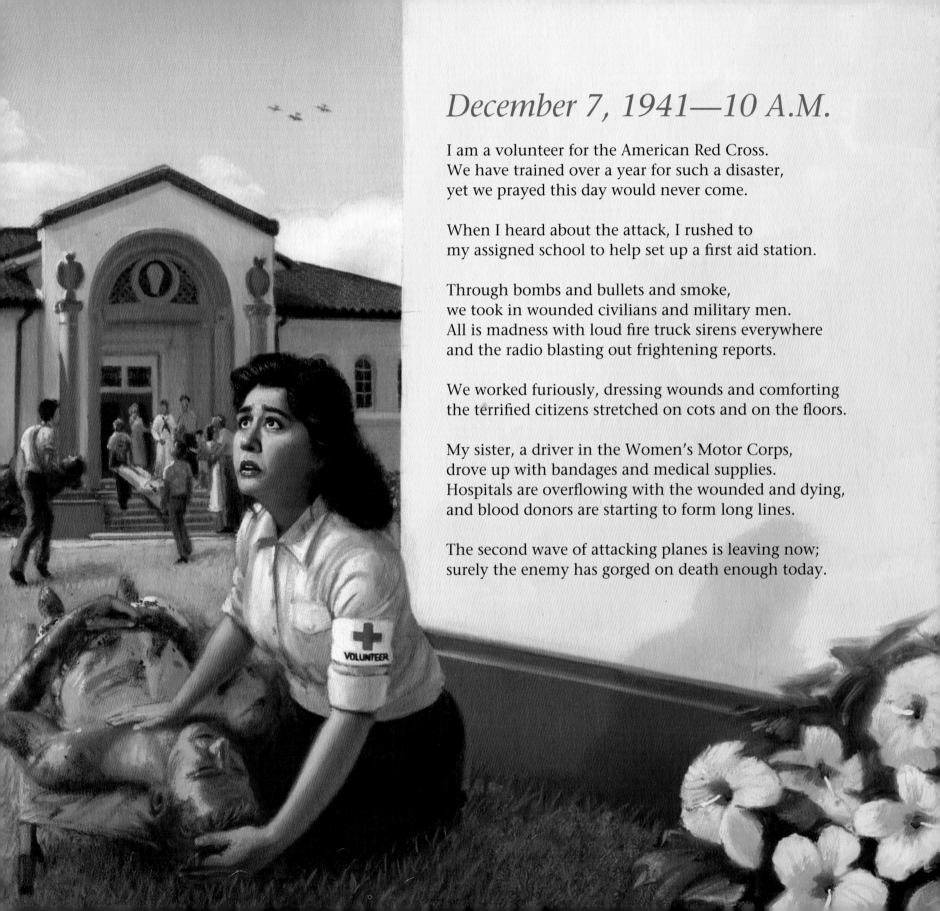

December 7, 1941—10 A.M.

I am a volunteer for the American Red Cross.
We have trained over a year for such a disaster,
yet we prayed this day would never come.

When I heard about the attack, I rushed to
my assigned school to help set up a first aid station.

Through bombs and bullets and smoke,
we took in wounded civilians and military men.
All is madness with loud fire truck sirens everywhere
and the radio blasting out frightening reports.

We worked furiously, dressing wounds and comforting
the terrified citizens stretched on cots and on the floors.

My sister, a driver in the Women's Motor Corps,
drove up with bandages and medical supplies.
Hospitals are overflowing with the wounded and dying,
and blood donors are starting to form long lines.

The second wave of attacking planes is leaving now;
surely the enemy has gorged on death enough today.

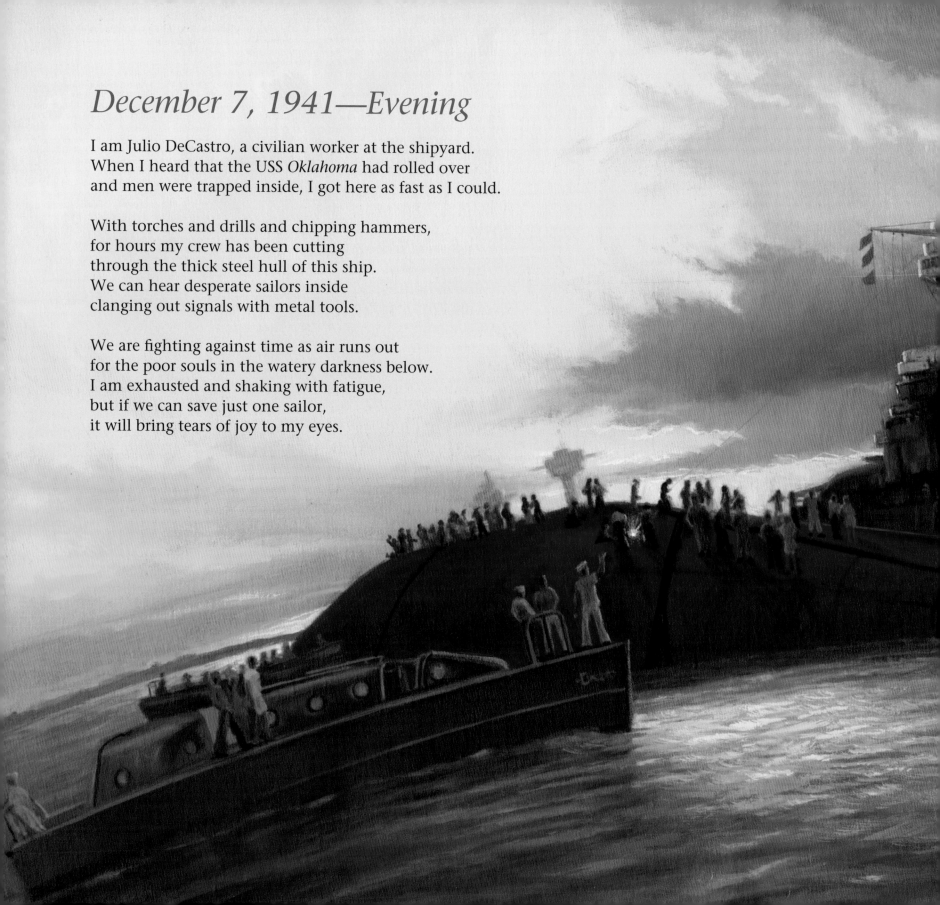

December 7, 1941—Evening

I am Julio DeCastro, a civilian worker at the shipyard.
When I heard that the USS *Oklahoma* had rolled over
and men were trapped inside, I got here as fast as I could.

With torches and drills and chipping hammers,
for hours my crew has been cutting
through the thick steel hull of this ship.
We can hear desperate sailors inside
clanging out signals with metal tools.

We are fighting against time as air runs out
for the poor souls in the watery darkness below.
I am exhausted and shaking with fatigue,
but if we can save just one sailor,
it will bring tears of joy to my eyes.

December 8, 1941

I am a Japanese-American, a *Nisei,*
born and raised in Honolulu.

After yesterday's attack on Pearl Harbor, my mother
took down the family scrolls and photo of the emperor,
and my father hung American flags in his shop windows
to let people know where our loyalties lie.

Our island is now under martial law;
schools are closed, businesses are shuttered,
and buses and the mail have stopped running.
At night a curfew is enforced and
windows must be covered in black.

Today we gathered around Pop's shortwave radio
to listen to Roosevelt's address to Congress
asking it to declare war on the Empire of Japan.
The president began with these solemn words:

"Yesterday, December 7, 1941,
—a date which will live in infamy—"

Tomorrow I'll join the Army and show the world
you can't push America around like this.

August 15, 1945

I am a widow filled with endless sorrow.
My husband died fighting on Okinawa;
my son perished in a kamikaze attack.

How full of pride and fervor was everyone's heart
with the success at Pearl Harbor more than three years ago;
how full of confidence for a victory in the Pacific.

Slowly our army and navy were shattered,
but leaders refused to throw down their swords
for that is not the *samurai* way.
American firebombs turned our houses
and factories into charred ruins;
Hiroshima and Nagasaki were bombed into oblivion,
yet still the honorable leaders said:
"We will give our last breath
for the Emperor and for Nippon."

Now the loud-speaker crackles
and people stand in stunned silence
as Emperor Hirohito speaks in the old language
of the imperial court, saying Japan will surrender.

At last it is over.

December 2001

My grandfather was a young sailor here back in 1941.
Today we rode out to the USS *Arizona* Memorial
to pay respects to those who lost their lives.

Grandpa's hands trembled as he cast
sweet white flowers onto the oily water.
A lot of old men were doing the same thing.
"It could have been me," I heard someone whisper.

We saw a gray-haired Japanese veteran
standing quietly to the side, head bowed low.
My grandfather spoke to the man a moment,
then they smiled and shook hands.

"Was that a Japanese pilot?" I asked. "From 1941?"

"Indeed it was," Grandpa said.
"He bombed my ship, the *Tennessee*."

"How can you be so nice to him?
Japan started that awful war."

"Yes, once we were bitter enemies," Grandpa said,
"but now our memories bind us together.
Now we are brothers of history."

Historical Note

On December 7, 1941, in a surprise dawn attack, a strike force of Japanese airplanes devastated the American Naval Fleet at Pearl Harbor, Hawaii, along with nearby army and marine installations and aircraft. More than 2,400 people were killed and more than 1,200 were wounded. This event caused the United States to enter World War II, the most destructive war in history. Although the attack surprised most Americans, events leading to that day had been transpiring for years and several warnings went unheeded.

In the 1930s war broke out in Europe, but the United States resisted involvement. In Japan, militant leaders such as General Hideki Tojo rose to power. They wanted to expand Japan's territories and to remove foreigners from Asia. In 1931, Japan invaded Manchuria, then China in 1937, causing the deaths of hundreds of thousands of civilians. The United States condemned Japan's actions but continued selling them raw materials needed for war, such as iron and oil. As Japan's aggression continued, the United Stated levied several trade embargoes.

In 1940 Japan signed the Tripartite Pact, becoming allies with Germany and Italy. In mid-1941, Japan moved troops into Indochina. The United States responded by banning all trade with Japan, including oil, and demanding that Japan withdraw its armies. Japanese envoys in Washington, D.C. continued negotiating for an agreement suitable to both sides.

The United States owned several territories in the Pacific, including the Hawaiian Islands, which had been annexed in 1898. At Pearl Harbor on Oahu Island, the United States had built a naval base and nearby army and marine installations, air fields, and ship-repair facilities. In May 1940, in a controversial move, President Roosevelt relocated the American Pacific Fleet from California to Pearl Harbor. Most Americans did not believe that Pearl Harbor was in jeopardy of attack, because it was almost 4,000 miles from Japan and was well-protected. Also, the shallow harbor thwarted submarine and torpedo attacks.

Desperate for raw materials to continue its war in China, Japan wanted to invade oil-rich Southeast Asia but knew such an act would cause war with the United States, Great Britain, and the Netherlands. Japan's best hope for success was to strike the first blow and destroy as many Pacific military installations as possible. In early 1941, Japanese Imperial Navy Admiral Isoroku Yamamoto proposed a risky plan for a surprise attack on Pearl Harbor, calling for the use of aircraft carriers traversing the rough winter waters of the North Pacific. The plan required improvised torpedoes that would work in shallow water and many hours of special training for the naval aviators. It called for absolute secrecy—only the highest ranking officials knew of the mission.

In the fall of 1941, US cryptologists in Hawaii intercepted several suspicious Japanese diplomatic and naval coded messages, but because Hawaii did not have a code-breaker machine, the unread messages were forwarded to Washington, D.C. However, Admiral Husband Kimmel, commander of the Pacific Naval Fleet, and Lt. General Walter Short, commander of the US Army in Hawaii, were never given these messages after they were decoded. Several messages strongly suggested that Pearl Harbor might be a target.

In late November, Washington D.C. finally sent a "war warning" to all the commanders in the Pacific saying that Japan might attack someplace soon, but Pearl Harbor was not specified. Instead, the alert told Lt. General Short to look out for sabotage from locals. In response, Short ordered the army airplanes to be grouped in the open so they could be easily guarded, and he also ordered ammunition to be locked up.

Diplomatic negotiations were disintegrating, so on November 26, the Japanese war fleet left the frigid Kuril Islands where they had gathered and advanced toward Hawaii under radio silence. The fleet, commanded by Vice-Admiral Chuichi Nagumo, included six carriers loaded with more than 400 aircraft, accompanied by battleships, destroyers, heavy cruisers, and fuel tankers. Submarines approached Hawaii from another route. On December 2, Nagumo received a coded message: "Climb Mount Niitaka 1208." The attack would proceed.

The Japanese war fleet stopped about 230 miles north of Pearl Harbor, out of range of American patrol planes. Before dawn on December 7, 1941, 350 Japanese airplanes began surging from the carriers in two waves made up of torpedo bombers, high-level bombers, dive bombers, and fighter planes. The submarines had already arrived at Pearl Harbor.

Around 4:00 a.m., a US minesweeper spotted a submarine and reported it to the USS *Ward,* a destroyer. Around 6:45 a.m., after intensive searching, the *Ward* fired upon and sank a Japanese midget-sub (a small sub that carried two men and two torpedoes) outside the harbor. This was reported to naval headquarters, but it did not reach Admiral Kimmel until it was too late.

At 7:02 a.m., the oscilloscope in a mobile radar station on Opana Point indicated a large number of planes coming from the north. The operators reported this to the officer on duty at the info center. This officer thought it was American B-17s flying in from California and due to arrive in Hawaii at 8:00 a.m., so he told the radar crew not to worry.

At 7:49 a.m., Captain Mitsuo Fuchida, leader of the Japanese air strike force, signaled the first wave's 183 planes to begin the attack. Each crew had been trained to bomb or torpedo or strafe a specific target. Below them the American fleet slept in Sunday silence. As the attack began, Fuchida sent a coded message to the flagship: *"Tora! Tora! Tora!"* meaning the attack was a successful surprise.

At 7:53 a.m., the first wave began bombing and strafing army bases and air fields. Aircraft on the ground at Wheeler, Kaneohe Bay, Ford Island, Ewa, Hickam, and Bellows were devastated. Only a few American pilots managed to get into the air. With ammunition locked away, soldiers could not immediately load the anti-aircraft guns.

Almost simultaneously, Japanese planes dropped bombs and launched torpedoes at Battleship Row. At first servicemen did not know what was happening. Many thought it was a practice drill, but when airplanes and ships began exploding, the loudspeakers crackled with: *"This is no drill!"*

The USS *Arizona* exploded after an armor-piercing bomb hit its ammunition magazine, killing 1,177 men. Fuel from the damaged ships leaked into the harbor and ignited. Many sailors swimming to shore were severely burned. The USS *Oklahoma* rolled over, trapping more than 400 men. Some sailors found pockets of air and tapped out signals. Civilian shipyard employees worked frantically with torches and pneumatic tools to cut through the thick steel hull, but only thirty-two men were rescued. Hospitals and schools overflowed with the wounded, including many civilians. Volunteers worked diligently to save lives.

The first attack lasted about thirty-five minutes. The second wave of 167 planes attacked around 9 a.m. By 10 a.m., the worst naval disaster in US history was over. All eight battleships were damaged, and four were sunk. Also destroyed or damaged were several destroyers, cruisers, and auxiliary vessels. The Navy lost 2,008 men; the Army lost 218 men; the Marines lost 109 men; and 49 civilians died. American aircraft losses included 169 destroyed and 159 damaged, while the Japanese lost twenty-nine planes and all five midget subs.

The next day, Congress declared war on Japan after hearing President Franklin Roosevelt's stirring address which began, *"Yesterday, December 7, 1941–a date which will live in infamy . . ."* FDR's speech was the most listened to radio broadcast in US history. On December 11, Japan's allies, Germany and Italy, declared war on the United States. Japan also attacked and conquered British, Dutch, and American possessions in Southeast Asia and the Pacific. But the three US aircraft carriers, the fuel storage tanks, and the dry docks at Pearl Harbor were unscathed. Consequently, six of the US battleships were repaired and put back into service.

Admiral Yamamoto was rumored to have said that the attack might "awaken a sleeping giant." Instead of demoralizing Americans, the attack united the nation. Unfortunately, 120,000 Japanese-Americans, two-thirds of whom were American citizens, were forced to leave their homes on the West coast and live in isolated, overcrowded internment camps.

For three and a half years, the US pushed the Japanese back, methodically destroying their navy in decisive battles such as Coral Sea, Midway, and Leyte Gulf. The last battle of the war occurred on Okinawa, only 400 miles from Japan.

By August 1945, the war in Europe was over and Americans were poised to invade Japan. Military and civilian deaths would be in the hundreds of thousands, yet the militant Japanese leaders would not surrender. To end the war, President Harry Truman approved the use of an atomic bomb on Hiroshima. When Japan still did not surrender, an atomic bomb was dropped on Nagasaki. Also, the Soviets invaded Japanese territory. Seeing the hopelessness, on August 15, Emperor Hirohito announced Japan's surrender.

In 1962, the ruined hulk of the USS *Arizona* became a national memorial and today is operated by the National Park Service. It stands as a reminder of that day of infamy when a sleeping giant was awakened.

Glossary

Boatswain—[bo'sun] a person in charge of a ship's maintenance and security

Cryptologist—a person who breaks secret codes

Embargo—a law prohibiting trade

Envoy—foreign diplomat such as an ambassador

Flagship—ship that carries the admiral commanding a fleet

Kamikaze—Japanese suicide attack, often by airplane

"Kate," "Val," and "Zero"—nicknames for Japanese airplanes

Nisei—American-born person whose parents are Japanese

Nippon—another name for Japan

Oscilloscope—instrument that projects electromagnetic waves on a screen

Quay—concrete structure to which a ship is moored

Rising Sun—the national symbol of Japan

Saboteur—an enemy agent or sympathizer who does damage

Samurai—ancient class of warriors dedicated to honor and loyalty

Strafe—to fire machine guns from a low flying airplane

Tarmac—paved, parking area near the airplane hangars

Torpedo—a motorized bomb designed to travel through water

Selected Bibliography

Conroy, Hilary and Harry Wray, eds. *Pearl Harbor Reexamined: Prologue to the Pacific War*. Honolulu: University of Hawaii Press, 1990.

Gannon, Michael V. *Pearl Harbor Betrayed*. New York: Henry Holt, 2001.

Iriye, Akira. *The Origins of the Second World War in Asia and the Pacific*. London: Longman, 1987.

_____. *Pearl Harbor and the Coming of the Pacific War*. New York: Bedford/St. Martins, 1999.

La Forte, Robert S. and Ronald E. Marcello. *Remembering Pearl Harbor*. Wilmington, Del.: Scholarly Resources, Inc., 1991.

Lord, Walter. *Day of Infamy*. New York: Holt, 1957.

Love, Robert W., ed. *Pearl Harbor Revisited*. New York: St. Martin's Press, 1995.

Prange, Gordon W. *At Dawn We Slept*. New York: Penguin Books, 1981.

_____ with Donald M. Goldstein and Katherine V. Dillon. *Pearl Harbor: The Verdict of History*. New York: McGraw-Hill, 1986.

_____ with Donald M. Goldstein and Katherine V. Dillon. *December 7, 1941*. New York: McGraw-Hill, 1988.

_____ with Donald M. Goldstein and Katherine V. Dillon. *God's Samurai: Lead Pilot at Pearl Harbor*. Washington, D.C.: Brassey's, 1990.

Stillwell, Paul. *Air Raid Pearl Harbor: Recollections of a Day of Infamy*. Annapolis, Md.: Naval Institute Press, 1981.

For Younger Readers

Denenberg, Barry. *Early Sunday Morning: The Pearl Harbor Diary of Amber Billows*. New York: Scholastic Dear America Series, 2001.

Duey, Kathleen. *American Diaries #18: Janey G. Blue–Pearl Harbor, 1941*. New York: Simon & Schuster, 2001.

Earle, Joan Zuber. *The Children of Battleship Row: Pearl Harbor 1940-1941*. Oakland, Calif.: RDR Books, 2002.

Houston, Jeanne Wakatsuki and James D. Houston. *Farewell to Manzanar*. New York: Random House, 1973.

Kudlinski, Kathleen V. *Pearl Harbor is Burning!* New York: Puffin Books, 1993.

Mazer, Harry. *Boy at War: A Novel of Pearl Harbor*. New York: Simon & Schuster, 2001.

Mochizuki, Ken. *Baseball Saved Us*. New York: Lee & Low, 1993.

Tanaka, Shelley. *Attack on Pearl Harbor*. New York: Hyperion Books, 2001.

Taylor, Theodore. *Air Raid Pearl Harbor!* San Diego, Calif.: Harcourt, Inc., 1991.

van der Vat, Dan. *Pearl Harbor: The Day of Infamy–An Illustrated History*. Toronto: Madison Press Books, 2001.

Wels, Susan. *Pearl Harbor: America's Darkest Day*. San Diego, Calif.: Tehabi Books, 2001.

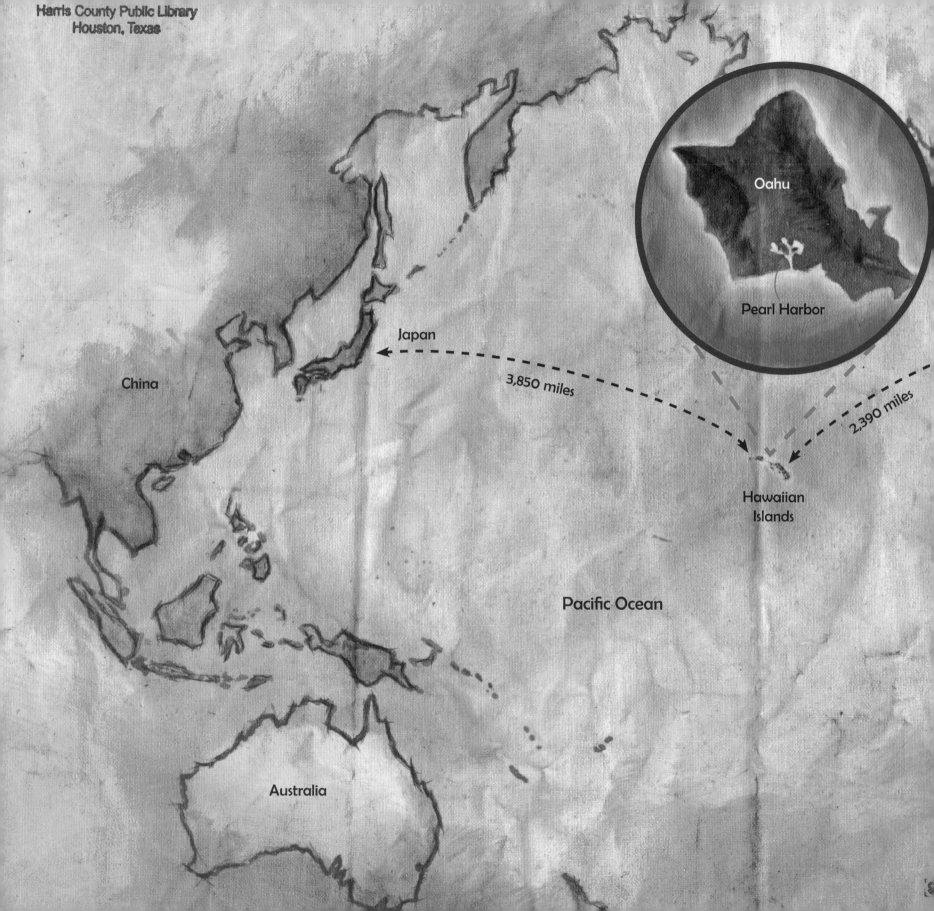

Oahu

Pearl Harbor

Japan

China

3,850 miles

2,390 miles

Hawaiian
Islands

Pacific Ocean

Australia